Printing

Rose Griffiths
Photographs by Peter Millard

A & C Black · London

A CIP catalogue record for this book is available
from the British Library
ISBN 0 7136 3628 9

A&C Black (Publishers) Ltd
35 Bedford Row, London, WC1R 4JH
© 1992 A&C Black (Publishers) Ltd

Acknowledgements

Mathematics consultant Mike Spooner

The photographer, author and publishers would
like to thank the following people whose help
and co-operation made this book possible:
the staff and pupils of Kenmont Primary School,
Jake Roberts, the Early Learning Centre.

Photograph on page 4 supplied by Noble Public Relations Ltd

Typeset by Rowland Phototypesetting Ltd,
Bury St Edmunds, Suffolk.
Printed and bound in Italy by L.E.G.O. Spa

All of these things have been printed.

Some things are printed by machine . . .

. . . and some things are printed by hand.

5

Can you see how I printed
each part of my picture?

6

These printing blocks
are made of wood.

I can use them again
and again.

How many elephants
have I printed?

Andy used four different
rubber stamps to make
a domino game.

How many different
dominoes can he print?

I'm printing different patterns
with this potato block.

Which is your favourite pattern?

Andy used his hand to make a print.

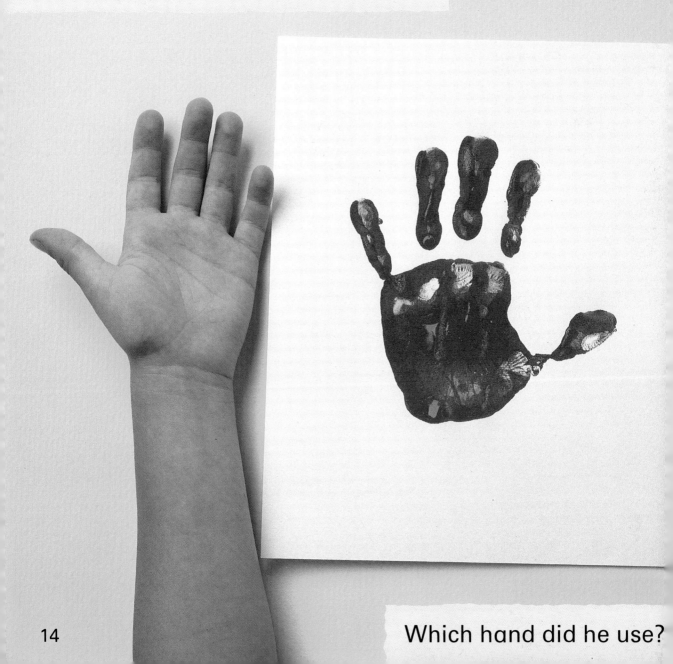

Which hand did he use?

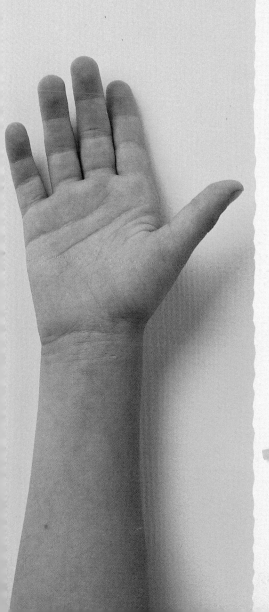

I'm going to print my initial.

Which side of the sponge
should I paint?

I made the letters
of my name from
pipe cleaners.

Which block will
print my name?

Rosa Rosa

Rosa Rosa

Rosa Rosa

Rosa Rosa

I can check with a mirror.

Andy used dots
to print his initials
on his book.

20

Our computer printer makes letters and pictures from tiny dots.

Look at all the things
we have printed.

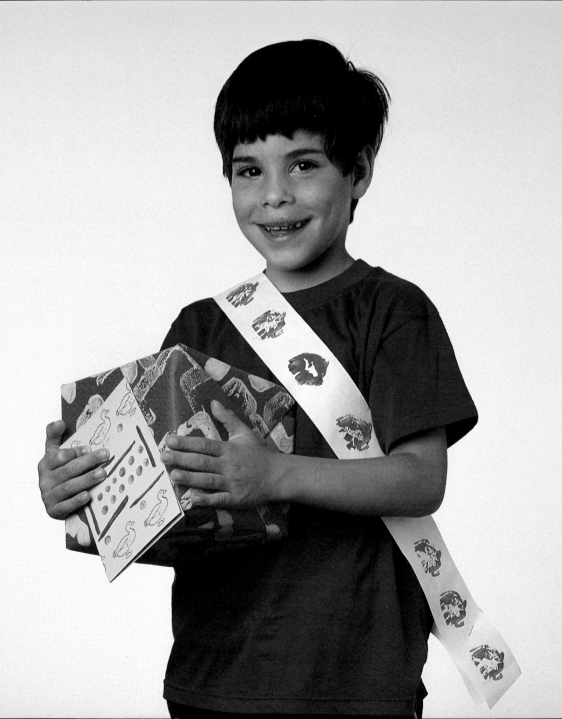

More things to do

1. Picture-matching game
Make this game to play on your own or with a friend. Cut out sixteen pieces of card, each about the size of a playing card. Choose four different rubber stamp pictures. Print one picture on four cards, and then another picture on four cards, until each picture is printed on four cards. Shuffle the cards and spread them all out, face down so you cannot see the pictures. When it's your go, turn over two cards. If they match, keep them. If they don't match, turn them back. How many pairs can you collect?

If you printed your cards with eight different pictures, would the game be easier or harder? What other matching games can you make using prints?

2. Printing blocks
You can make your own printing blocks from pipe cleaners or shapes cut from a kitchen sponge. Glue your pipe cleaners or sponge on to thick card or a small piece of wood and leave it to dry. Lean your paper on newspaper. Use a paintbrush to apply the paint to the sponge shape or pipe cleaners and press the block on to your paper. Try to make different patterns. You could make a paper fan and then print over each fold to make a pattern or you could make some wrapping paper.

Notes for parents and teachers

As you read this book with children, these notes will help you to explain the mathematical ideas behind the different activities.

Printing all around us   Pages 2, 3, 4, 5, 22, 23
Printing enables many copies of the same thing to be made. Copies printed by machine are usually exactly the same as one another, but copies printed by hand are usually more varied. Children can look at printed fabrics and wallpaper to find the places where the pattern repeats, or at two copies of the same book to check that they are the same.

Matching and counting   Pages 6, 7, 8, 9
A print does not always look exactly like the object which has been used to print it. Children can make a collection of objects with which to print. It is also valuable for children to talk about how they printed their own pictures and to analyse each others' pictures.

When children check the number of times they have printed something, a meaningful context for counting and simple arithmetic is provided. For example, "I've printed seven rabbits and I need ten altogether. How many more must I print?"

Combinations   Pages 10, 11
With four pictures you can make sixteen different dominoes, since each picture can be printed with four others, including itself. Most children will approach the problem of finding out how many combinations there are by making a few dominoes in a fairly random order, and then trying to think of more. Don't be tempted to step in too soon. It's more useful if children realise for themselves the need for a logical system.

How many different dominoes can be made with five different pictures, or six, or seven?

Translation and rotation   Pages 12, 13
A translation is the name given to the movement of a shape from its original position to a new position, without turning it or changing its size. On page 13, the top two and bottom right patterns are made in this way. The fourth pattern is made using rotation, or turning, and then translation. Most children and adults find it more difficult to copy or continue a pattern using rotation.

Reflection   Pages 14, 15, 16, 17, 18, 19
A printed image is the reverse of the image on the printing block. If you write your name on paper and look at it in the mirror, or write it on tracing paper and turn the paper over, you can see how a printing block of your name would look. When some letters are turned over or reflected, they do not look different. This is because they have a line of symmetry themselves, for example the capital letters I, M, O, V, W and X. Children who frequently reverse letters accidentally may find it helpful to have an alphabet to refer to when looking at their names in the mirror.

Computer printing   Pages 20, 21
Many computers use dot matrix printers. When you look closely at dot matrix printing, you can see that the letters and shapes are made from lots of dots printed next to each other. Children can use a magnifying glass to see this. They can look at particular letters to see if the printer always uses the same array of dots to print an 'a' for example. Some pictures in books and newspapers are printed from dots.